To my mother, for the greatest gift

— her unconditional love.

The more a child becomes aware
of a mother's willingness to listen,
the more a mother will begin to hear.

W ho takes the child by the hand,
takes the mother by the heart.

— Danish Proverb

$$\text{\Large{\textbf{\textit{(decorative flourish)}}}}$$

All that I am or hope to be,
I owe to my mother.

— A. Lincoln

God could not be everywhere,
so therefore he made mothers.

— Hebrew Proverb

Parents of teens and parents of babies
have something in common.
They spend a great deal of time
trying to get their kids to talk.

—Paul Swets

When we see great men and women,
we give credit to their mothers.

— Charlotte Perkins Gilman

No matter how old a mother is
she watches her middle-aged children
for signs of improvement.

— Florida Scott-Maxwell

We cannot put mothering into a formula
and come up with a person
who has the special feeling for your child
that you do.

— Dr. Sally E. Shaywitz

Dear Mother —
You know that nothing can ever change
what we have always been
and will always be to each other.

— Franklin Roosevelt

Mother:
The person who *sits* up with you
when you are sick,
and *puts* up with you
when you are well.

∿⦿∿

There is no friendship, no love,
like that of the mother for the child.

— Henry Ward Beecher

Who ran to help me when I fell,
And would some pretty story tell,
Or kiss the place to make it well?
My Mother.

—Anne Taylor

Reasoning with a child if fine,
if you can reach the child's reason
without destroying your own.

— John Mason Brown

P arents must get across the idea that,
"I love you always,
but sometimes I do not love
your behavior."

— Amy Vanderbilt

I never understood the obstacles
my mother faced,
until I became one.
I love my mother's memory
now more than ever.

$$\text{\tiny ⦅◖◗⦆}$$

Other things may change us,
but we start and end with the family.

— Anthony Brandt

The best gift a mother can give her child
is the gift of herself.

Mothers are the most unselfish,
the most responsible
people in the world.

— Bernard M. Baruch

For the hand that rocks the cradle
is the hand that rules the world.

— William Ross Wallace

Children who despise their parents
do so until about age forty,
when they suddenly become like them.

You can multiply all the relations of life,
have more than one sister or brother;
in the course of events,
have more than one wife,
but you never can have but one mother!

There is only one pretty child
in the world,
and every mother has it.

— English Proverb

Perhaps nobody
becomes more competent
in hitting a moving target
than a mother spoon feeding a baby.

It was when I had my first child
that I understood how much
my mother loved me.

She is just an extraordinary mother
and a gentle person.
I depended on her for everything...
I watched her become a strong person,
and that had an enormous influence
on me.

— Rosalynn Carter

A child's hand in yours —
what tenderness and power it arouses.
You are instantly the very touchstone
of wisdom and strength.

— Marjorie Holms

Rejecting things
because they are old-fashioned
would rule out the sun and the moon —
and a mother's love.

A mother's heart
is a baby's most beautiful dwelling.

— Ed Dussault

Children are the anchors
that hold a mother to life.

—Sophocles

Truth, which is important to a scholar,
has got to be concrete.
And there's nothing more concrete
than dealing with babies,
burps, bottles and frogs.

— Jeane Kirkpatrick

Nothing else will ever make you
as happy or as sad,
as proud or as tired,
as motherhood.

— Elia Parsons

If evolution really works,
how come mothers
have only two hands?

— Ed Dussault

$\mathcal{C} \mathfrak{D}$

In motherhood
there's so much to learn,
so much to give
and although the learning gets less
with each child,
the giving never does.

— Marguerite Kelly

You don't choose your family.
They are God's gift to you,
as you are to them.

— Desmond Tutu

A baby enters your home
and makes so much noise
for twenty years you can hardly stand it —
then departs,
leaving the house so silent
you think you'll go mad.

— Dr. J. A. Holmes

$\mathcal{CD}$

An important thing for parents
to teach their children
is how to get along without them.

— F. Clark

Be kind to thy mother,
for when thou were young,
who loved thee so fondly as she?

— Margaret Courtney

A mother's love is patient and forgiving
when all others are forsaking,
and it never fails or falters,
even though the heart is breaking.

— Helen Steiner Rice

The imprint of the mother
remains forever
on the life of the child.

A mother should be like a quilt —
keep the children warm
but don't smother them.

Give a little love to a child
and you get a great deal back.

— John Ruskin

You can be sure it's her first-born
if a mother cries
when her youngster starts school.

A mother's patience
is like a tube of toothpaste —
it's never quite gone.

Parents learn a lot from their children
about coping with life.

— Muriel Spark

A mother is not a person to lean on
but a person to make leaning
unnecessary.

— Dorothy Fischer

꧁ ꧂

A man loves his sweetheart the most,
his wife the best,
but his mother the longest.

— Irish Proverb

L is the first gift,
love is the second,
and understanding the third.

A woman who can cope
with the terrible twos
can cope with anything.

Loving a child doesn't mean
giving in to all his whims;
to love him is to bring out
the best in him,
to teach him to love what is difficult.

— Nadia Boulanger

There is no influence so powerful
as that of the mother.

— Sarah Josepha Hale

When you are a mother,
you are never really alone
in your thoughts.
You are connected to your child
and to all those who touch your lives.
A mother always has to think twice,
once for herself
and once for her child.

— Sophia Loren

All the earth,
though it were full of kind hearts,
is but a desolation and deserted place
to a mother
when her only child is absent.

— Elizabeth Gaskell

We never know the love of the parent
until we become parents ourselves.

— Henry Ward Beecher

Being a mother, as far as I can tell,
is a constantly evolving process
of adapting to the needs of your child
while also changing and growing
as a person in your own right.

— Deborah Insel

A wonderful motto for teens and parents
is to never needlessly harm
the respect of another.

— Dr. Kay Kuzma

The mother is the medium
which the primitive infant
transforms himself
into a socialized human being.

— Beata Rank

A little child, a limber self.
Singing, dancing to itself...
Makes such a vision to the sight,
as fills a mother's eyes with light.

Any mother could perform the jobs
of several air traffic controllers
with ease.

— Lisa Alther

What a mother says to her children
is not heard by the world,
but it will be heard by posterity.

Cleaning your house
while your kids are still growing
is like shoveling the walk
before it stops snowing.

— Phyllis Diller

When you are dealing with a child,
keep all your wits about you,
and sit on the floor.

— A. O'Malley

Loving a child is a circular business
the more you give, the more you get,
the more you want to give.

— Penelope Leach

Seeing you sleeping peacefully
on your back
among your stuffed ducks,
bears and basset hounds
would remind me
that no matter how good
the next day might be,
certain moments were gone forever.

— Joan Baez

While you can quarrel
with a grown-up,
how can you quarrel
with a newborn baby
who has stretched out his little arms
for you to pick him up?

— Maria Von Trapp

Mommy herself has told us
that she looked upon us more as her friends
than her daughters.
Now that is all very fine,
but still, a friend can't take a mother's place.
I need my mother as an example
which I can follow,
I want to be able to respect her.

—Anne Frank

There's a lot more to being a woman
than being a mother,
but there's a lot more to being a mother
than most people suspect.

— Roseanne Arnold

There is nothing more thrilling
in this world, I think,
than having a child that is yours,
and yet is mysteriously a stranger.

— Agatha Christie

The phrase "working mother"
is redundant.

— Jane Sellman

I n bringing up children,
what good mothers
instinctively feel like doing
for their babies
is usually best after all.

— Benjamin Spock

W e are together, my child and I.
Mother and child, yes,
but sisters really,
against whatever denies us
all that we are.

— Alice Walker

For me motherhood has been
the one true, great,
and wholly successful romance.
It is the only love I have known
that is expansive
and that could have stretched
to contain with equal passion
more than one object.

Children are such sticky things,
'specially after tea.

— E. F. Benson

Words which explode
at an impressionable moment
in the life of a young child,
can shape an entire personality.

— Gordon MacDonald

Other Titles by Great Quotations, Inc

Hard Covers

African American Excellence
Ancient Echoes
Attitudes of Success
Behold the Golfer
Celebrating Friendship
Commanders In Chief
Dare to Dream
First Ladies
Graduation
Golf
Good Lies for Ladies
Heartfelt Affection
Improving With Age
Inspirations for Success
Inspired Thoughts
I Thought of You Today
Journey to Success
Just Between Friends
Keys to Achieving Your Goals

Lasting Impressions
My Dear Mom
My Husband, My Love
Never Ever Give Up
Peace Be With You
Seeds of Inspiration
Seeds of Knowledge
Sharing Our Love
Sharing the Season
Smile Now
Teddy Bears
The Essence of Music
The Passion of Chocolate
The Perfect Brew
The Power of Inspiration
There's No Place Like Home
The Spirit of Christmas
Thoughts From Great Women

Great Quotations, Inc.
1967 Quincy Court
Glendale Heights, IL 60139 USA
Phone: 630-582-2800 Fax: 630-582-2813
http://www. greatquotations.com

Other Titles by Great Quotations, Inc

Paperbacks

A Servant's Heart
A Teacher is Better Than Two Books
I'm Not Over the Hill
Life's Lessons
Looking for Mr. Right
Midwest Wisdom
Mommy & Me
Mother, I Love You
Motivating Quotes
Mrs. Murphy's Laws
Mrs. Webster's Dictionary
Only A Sister
Parenting 101
Pink Power
Romantic Rhapsody
Social Disgraces
Stress or Sanity
The Mother Load
The Other Species
The Secret Languauge of Men
The Secret Languauge of Women
The Secrets in Your Name
Teenage of Insanity
Touch of Friendship
Wedding Wonders
Words From the Coach

Perpetual Calendars

365 Reasons to Eat Chocolate
All Star Quotes
Always Remember Who Loves You
A Touch of Kindness
Coffee Breaks
Extraordinary Leaders
Generations
I'm a Little Stressed
I Think My Teacher Sleeps at School
Kid Stuff
My Friend & Me
Never Never Give Up
Older Than Dirt
Secrets of a Successful Mom
Shopoholic
Sweet Dreams
Teacher Zone
Tee Times
The Dog Ate My Car Keys
The Essence of Great Women
The Heart That Loves
The Honey Jar
Winning Words